1966 Mercury Cyclone GT
A POWERFUL & RARE MERCURY FOR UNDER $10K

Text by Joe Babiasz, photos by Brendan Moran

Ford's Mercury division has been synonymous with mid-price luxury transportation. But few know that the division that gave us the "Breezeway" retracting rear window also built one of America's first factory muscle cars. In 1958, Mercury released a dealer-installed Super Marauder tri-power option for its 430 cubic-inch big-block engine. Adding tri-power bumped up advertised horsepower to an incredible 400, and helped contribute to making Mercury a performance powerhouse. The option was short lived and by the early-1960s Mercury took a

back seat to Ford, their lower priced cousin, in the manufacturing of tire-melting performance cars.

By 1966, Mercury was once again anxious to get back into the muscle car arena. Using the midsize Comet platform, engineers put their collective heads together to develop the Comet Cyclone and Cyclone GT. The standard Cyclone included all the visuals necessary to identify it as a muscle car, but powertrains were limited to a 289 cubic-inch small-block and a 265 or 275-horsepower, 390 cubic-inch engine, depending on the transmission ordered. A two-barrel

carburetor topped the base Cyclone 390. While providing adequate performance, it simply wasn't enough to keep up with other factory muscle cars of the time. For enthusiasts who wanted neck-snapping performance, ordering a Cyclone GT was a necessity.

Under the Cyclone GT's hood rested Ford's 335-horsepower, 390 FE engine. This powerhouse included a Holley four-barrel carburetor mounted on a cast iron intake manifold. Its 10.5:1 compression ratio required premium fuel, and dual exhausts were standard equipment. An engine

"Under the Cyclone GT's hood rested Ford's 335-horsepower, 390 FE engine. This powerhouse included a Holley four-barrel carburetor mounted on a cast iron intake manifold."

being a performance vehicle. From the side, a special identification stripe ran across the lower body section. Simple horizontal taillamps rested in the rear tail panel.

All GT models included bucket seats, heavy-duty suspension, body striping, special wheels, and dual exhausts. Transmission availability was limited to a floor mounted standard three-speed manual, four-speed manual, or three-speed automatic.

The Comet Cyclone GT wasn't the hit the Mercury division had hoped for, selling only 15,970 during the model year. Perhaps it was the additional cost of buying a Mercury, or perhaps the stigma of believing a Mercury wasn't a real performance car. However, time has validated the Cyclone GT as a true performance car, and today it is a highly sought after muscle car for Ford and Mercury enthusiasts.

Special thanks to Melvin Benzaquen at Classic Restorations and car owner Geoff Malloy for allowing us to shoot this Cyclone GT.

dress-up kit finished off the under-hood niceties. All GTs were equipped with a 3.25:1 axle unless otherwise specified.

To improve ride quality and interior space for 1966, the wheel-base was increased two inches, to 116. Overall vehicle length was stretched to 203 inches, adding seven inches to the 1965 speci-fications. Body width was also increased to add additional shoulder room. Doors had curved glass and for the first time, air conditioning was a factory-installed option. A pad-ded dash and seatbelts were stan-

dard. New options for 1966 were power windows and a two-way power seat. An improved heater and sound-deadening package provided additional comfort to passengers.

Outside, the Cyclone GT was nearly a mirror image of Ford's Fairlane with a slab-sided body, a front end with dual stacked head-lamps, and a wide grille split hori-zontally by a body colored division bar. All GTs included a standard fiberglass hood with dual non-func-tional scoops. While it didn't add any horsepower, the hood certainly added to the visual effect of the GT

SPECIFICATIONS

Number built – 15,970

Construction – Unibody

Engine – 390 cubic-inch V-8

Power/Torque – 390 cubic-inch V-8, 335 horsepower, 427 lb-ft torque

Transmissions – Three-speed manual, four-speed manual, three-speed automatic

Suspension front – Single lower control arm, A-type upper control arm, independent coil springs

Suspension rear – Semi-elliptical leaf springs with four leafs

Steering – Re-circulating ball and nut

Brakes – Front disc, rear drum

Length/width/height – 203/73.8/54.3 inches

Wheelbase – 116 inches

Weight – 3,374 lbs.

0-60 mph/quarter mile – 6.6 seconds, 15.2 seconds at 90 mph (*Car Life*, April 1966)

Top speed – 120 mph (*Car Life*, April 1966)

MPG – 10.1 mpg (*Car Life* road test)

Price – MSRP - $3,152; Today – $5,625 - $17,100

FUEL FOR THOUGHT

- Mercury's premium midsize muscle car
- Convertibles are rare with only 2,158 produced
- 390's oil capacity reduced by one quart, to four
- All GT models included engine dress-up kit
- Available with optional nine-inch television

"Indy" 500 discovers Mercury Cyclone GT!

"Performance Car of the Year" Named Pace Car For Memorial Day 500

"Performance Car of the Year"

ENGINE

Ford's FE block was reliable and dependable, but didn't perform on par with GM's and Chrysler's big-blocks. The FE later grew into the renowned 428 Cobra Jet.

HANDLING

Typical of most intermediates of the time, the Comet was best suited for straight-line acceleration. Cornering was improved over the 1965 model, with longer rear leaf springs and a stiffer front suspension. Those cars equipped with 390s had the curse of a heavy front end, causing excessive leaning in corners.

STRONG POINTS

- Unique
- Excellent performance
- Low production numbers
- Room for five

WEAK POINTS

- It's a Mercury
- Un-restored vehicles can have rust issues
- NOS and aftermarket parts somewhat difficult to find
- Performance not on par with other factory muscle cars

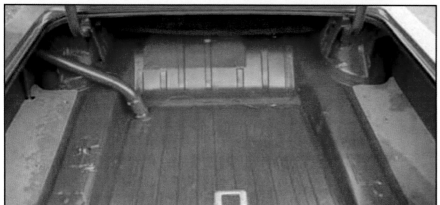

WHAT TO PAY

1966 MERCURY CYCLONE GT

- **MSRP – $3,152**
- **Low – $5,625**
- **Average – $10,300**
- **High – $17,100**

Based on NADA prices.

INSURANCE COST

Insurance cost is $136/year for a $10,300 1966 Mercury Cyclone GT. This is based on 3,000 miles per year of pleasure driving.

Based on a quote from Heacock Classic Car Insurance www.heacockclassic.com

PARTS PRICES

- Front floor pan section at footwell $119.95
- Carpet $142.50
- Power brake conversion kit $399.95
- Radiator $494.95
- Valve covers $64.95
- Gas tank $269.95

Based on information from Dearborn Classics 800-252-7427 www.dearbornclassics.com

VEHICLE CATEGORY

Many Cyclones are used on a semi-regular basis. They go to weekly cruise nights and are also shown at local shows. Few are trailered to events. While not as big as other groups, the Comet Cyclone GT enthusiasts are just as enthusiastic.

BOOKS

- *Mercury Comet & Cyclone Limited Edition Extra 1960-1975* **by R. M. Clarke**
- *Standard Catalog of American Muscle Cars 1960-1972* **by John Gunnell**
- *Mercury Muscle Cars (Musclecar Color History)* **by David Newhardt**
- *1966 Comet, Falcon, Fairlane and Mustang Shop Manual* **by Ford Motor Company**
- *Muscle Cars Field Guide: American Supercars 1960-2000* **by John Gunnell**

WEBSITES

www.mustangsandmore.com
www.musclecarclub.com
www.fordcarz.com
www.fordmuscle.com

ALTERNATIVE

1966 Buick Skylark Gran Sport

Number built – 13,816

0-60/quarter-mile – 7.6 seconds, 14.1 seconds at 95 mph

Top speed – 115 mph est.

Price – MSRP - $3,019; Today – $7,850 - $22,200

ALTERNATIVE

1966 Chevelle SS 396

Number built – 72,272

0-60/quarter-mile – 7.9 seconds, 14.6 seconds at 99 mph

Top speed – 120 mph est.

Price – MSRP - $2,776; Today – $12,900 - $42,000

REVIEW

The Cyclone GT was Mercury's version of a factory hot rod. It established Ford's premium division as a contributor to the glory days of performance cars.

1969 Chevelle SS 396
STILL FAST, STILL UNDER $20K

Text by Joe Babiasz, photos by Ryan Merrill

The year was 1969 and the Big Three, along with American Motors, were doling out horsepower like free candy in a candy store. But it was General Motors who was the volume leader of muscle car sales. The reason was simple: Chevrolet, Buick, Oldsmobile, and Pontiac each had something unique to offer customers. Yet it was Chevrolet who led the pack. And while Chevrolet's mid-size Chevelle SS 396 shared its platform with the 442, GTO, and Gran Sport, it–along with the rest of the GM lineup–had its own personality.

The Chevelle body was in its second year of production. A new grille with a horizontal bar separating the upper and lower section gave a wider look to the front end. Parking lamps were moved inboard into the center bumper opening. The body side molding was eliminated and replaced by an optional body side stripe. Larger taillamps and a blacked out center panel gave the rear end a more aggressive look.

For 1969, the Super Sport became an option package, RPO Z25, rather than a unique model as it was in 1968. The SS 396 package included a mild mannered 325-horsepower 396 cubic-inch V-8, three-speed manual transmis-

sion, domed hood, black accented grille, power front disc brakes, wide oval tires, and special suspension system. Buyers were required to hand over an additional $347.60 for the pleasure of ordering the option.

Inside, the Super Sport was comfortable but not luxurious. The dash sported twin round gauges centered above the steering column. A vinyl-covered front bench seat was standard equipment, but Strato-bucket seats could be selected from the option list. The seat cover design was slightly changed from the previous year. Nineteen sixty-nine was the first year for headrests, beating

the January 1970 federal require-
ment by about four months.

All Super Sports were powered
by Chevrolet's big-block. The base
325-horse engine, RPO L35, provided more than adequate performance along with the ability to be
ordered with air conditioning. For
those wanting more performance,
the 350-horsepower version was
available as RPO L34. Added performance pieces gave the Chevelle
improved performance, yet it was
mild enough for work-time traffic.
Buyers could choose from two versions of the 375-horse engine. The
primary difference was that the L89
included aluminum heads, shaving

about 100 pounds from the weight
of the vehicle. While not on the
official option list, a 425 horsepower, 427 cubic-inch powerhouse was
available but dealers were required
to place the order via the Central
Office Production Order (COPO).

The base transmission was a
three-speed manual. Additionally,
three versions of the Muncie four-
speed were available. The wide-
ratio M20 provided the best package for the street. The close-ratio
M21 kept the engine closer to its
torque curve, and the close-ratio
M22 was the ultimate if serious
drag racing was the owner's goal.
Chevrolet's two-speed Powerglide

was canceled for 1969 and
replaced with the stout three-speed
Turbo HydraMatic trans.

Considering the long list of available performance and comfort
options, the Super Sport catered to
the masses, whether they wanted
simple, low-cost performance or
high-end luxury combined with performance. By the end of the model
year over 86,000 were sold, making the Super Sport a bona-fide
success for Chevrolet.

Photos courtesy of NAHC

SPECIFICATIONS

Number built – 86,307

Construction – Body-on-frame

Engines – (4) 396 cubic-inch V-8, 427 cubic-inch V-8 (special order COPO)

Power/Torque – 396 cubic-inch V-8, 325 horsepower, 410 lb-ft torque, 396 cubic-inch V-8, 350 horsepower, 415 lb-ft torque, 396 cubic-inch V-8, 375 horsepower, 415 lb-ft torque, 396 cubic-inch V-8, 375 horsepower, 415 lb-ft torque (L89), 427 cubic-inch V-8, 425 horsepower, 460 lb-ft torque (COPO)

Transmissions – Three-speed manual, four-speed manual, three-speed automatic

Suspension front – Independent, short arm-long arm (SLA), coil springs and anti-sway bar

Suspension rear – Live axle with upper and lower control arms, coil springs

Steering – Re-circulating ball, 20.4:1 ratio

Brakes – Power front disc, rear drum

Length/width/height – 196.9/76.0/52.8 inches

Wheelbase – 112 inches

Weight – 3,335 lbs.

0-60 mph/quarter-mile – 7.6 seconds, 15.4 seconds at 92 mph (*Motor Trend*, January 1969)

Top speed – 115 mph est.

MPG – 8.6-11.8 mpg

Price – MSRP - $3,020; Today – $16,400 - $36,000

FUEL FOR THOUGHT

- Axle ratios ranged from 2.56:1 to 4.88:1

- L89 aluminum head option cost $647.75 (400 sold)

- Produced in five U.S. plants plus one in Canada

- Head restraints could be deleted until 12/31/68 (774 did)

ENGINE

Chevrolet's big-block was designed for high performance. The base 325-horse engine came with a cast crank and two-bolt mains. The 350- and 375-horse engines included a forged crank. All 375-horse engines included four-bolt mains.

HANDLING

The four corner coil spring ride was relatively soft for a muscle car and pushing it into hard turns proved to be a difficult–if not a near impossible–task. The optional F41 suspension added a rear anti-sway bar that improved its cornering ability.

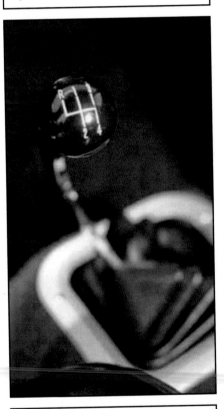

STRONG POINTS

- An iconic performance vehicle
- Reasonably priced after-market parts
- Substantial production means adequate availability

WEAK POINTS

- Many have been used and abused
- Easy to clone
- Less popular than the 1970 Chevelle SS

WHAT TO PAY

1969 CHEVELLE SS 396

- **MSRP – $3,020**
- **Low – $16,400**
- **Average – $21,600**
- **High – $36,000**

Based on prices from NADA.

INSURANCE COST

Insurance cost is $196/year for a $21,600 1969 Chevelle SS 396. This is based on 3,000 miles per year of pleasure driving.

Based on a quote from Heacock Classic Car Insurance, www.heacockclassic.com

PARTS PRICES

- Super Sport grille kit $399.95
- Radiator $459.95
- Fuel tank $119.95
- Door skin $152.95
- Windshield $168.95
- Leather seat upholstery $1,116.95

Based on information from Original Parts Group 800-243-8355 www.opgi.com

Special thanks to Rick Treworgy and his staff at Muscle Car City in Punta Gorda, FL for allowing us to photograph this Chevelle. To learn more about this massive museum, please call 941-575-5959 or visit www.musclecarcity.net

VEHICLE CATEGORY

While very rare COPO Chevelles stay hidden away in heated garages, Super Sport owners enjoy driving their vehicles on a semi-regular basis. National Chevelle clubs provide opportunities to show off Chevrolet's mid-size muscle car to the masses.

BOOKS

- *Chevelle* **by Mike Mueller**
- *Chevelle SS Restoration Guide* **by Paul Herd**
- *Chevelle and SS 1964-1972* **by R.M. Clarke**
- *Chevy SS: 50 Years of Super Sport* **by Robert Genat**

WEBSITES

www.chevellestuff.com
www.chevelles.net
www.chevelleforum.net
www.devotedtochevelles.com

REVIEW

The Chevelle SS 396 was then, as it is today, a highly sought after performance car. With a plethora of powertrains and crisp body lines, it remains a head turner at traffic lights and cruise nights alike. High horse-power versions are commanding extraordinary prices at auctions.

ALTERNATIVE
1969 Buick Gran Sport 400

Number built – 8,132

0-60/quarter-mile – 7.7 seconds, 15.9 seconds at 89 mph

Top speed – 115 mph est.

Price – **MSRP - $3,308;**
Today – $11,500 - $34,100

ALTERNATIVE
1969 Pontiac GTO

Number built – 65,454

0-60/quarter-mile – 7.2 seconds, 14.9 seconds at 98 mph

Top speed – 108 mph

Price – **MSRP - $3,293;**
Today – $12,100 - $47,100

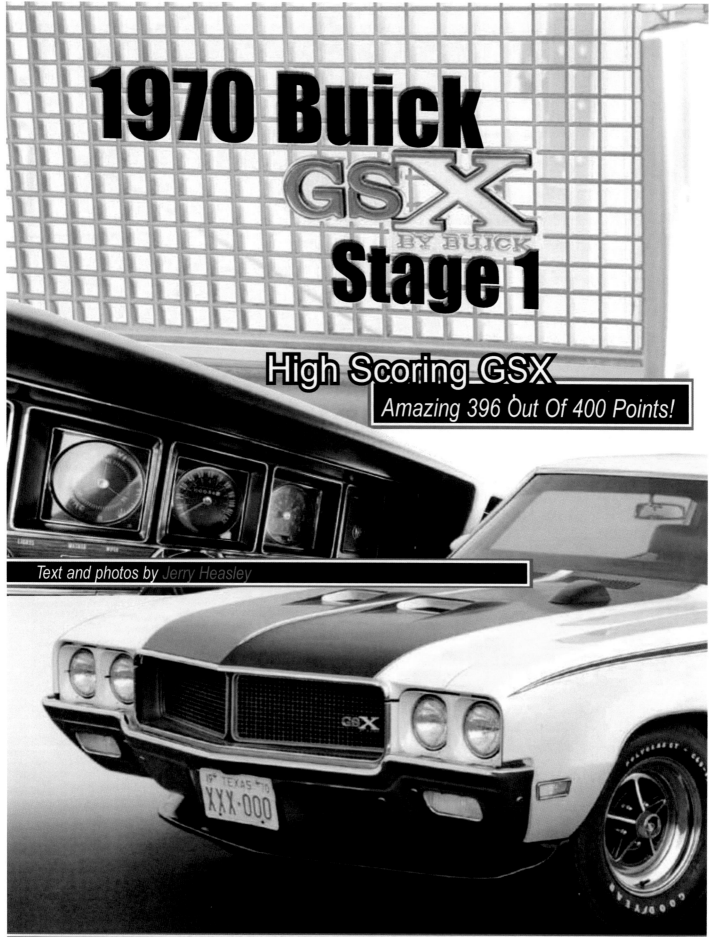

1970 Buick

GSX
BY BUICK

Stage 1

High Scoring GSX

Amazing 396 Out Of 400 Points!

Text and photos by Jerry Heasley

TEXAS '70
XXX·000

Buick was shooting for the stars in 1970 with their limited edition GSX. With 510 lb-ft of torque, the Stage 1 tune of the monstrous 455 V-8 lays claim to the highest ever for a classic muscle car.

Apparently, the brass at the #2 division of General Motors knew what they were doing when they limited the colors of this special edition muscle Buick to Apollo White and Saturn Yellow. Apollo was an Olympian god in both Greek and Roman mythology. Saturn, of course, is one of the planets in our solar system, as well as a Roman god.

When *Car Review* magazine first published their "50 Fastest Muscle Cars" list in 1984, it surprised Mopar fans with its #3 ranking of the GSX with Stage 1 455. Just two other classics were faster down the quarter mile. Number one was the lightweight and infamous 427 Cobra, of extremely limited production and just barely a street legal production car. Number two was another two-seat sports car, the 1966 Corvette with a 425hp 427. Buick, with a 13.38 @ 105.5 mph, proved faster than any other mid-sized or pony car from the 1960s/1970s. Road testers clipped off these times on street tires.

Buick fans had known all along how fast their muscle Buicks were. Luxury, however, had been Buick's calling card for decades. The nail head V-8s of the 1950s and early 1960s were known for their small valves and decent fuel economy. When muscle cars

The 455 Stage 1 boasts the highest torque rating ever on a classic muscle car. The 510 lb-ft of torque is King Kong for muscle cars of the 1964-1972 era. Interestingly enough, the standard 455, which was the base engine on the 1970 GSX, also produced 510 lb-ft of torque. Of the 678 Buick GSXs built in 1970, 400 had the Stage 1 455, and the balance of 278 had the standard 455. The Stage 1 added $115 to the cost of the base 455, quite a bargain. The scoops are open to ram air to the Rochester four barrel via twin scoops that seal to the underside of the hood.

The GSX package cost an additional $1195. In addition to the stripes, front and rear spoilers, a hood tach and Buick Rallye wheel (chromed), the GSX included mechanical upgrades of heavy-duty cooling, stiffer shocks, front/rear sway bars, and power front disc brakes.

became popular with Pontiac's GTO in 1964, soon Buick, same as Pontiac, fitted their own mid-sized Skylark with high output big blocks. Oldsmobile had their 4-4-2, Pontiac had their GTO, Chevrolet had their SS, while Buick had their GS, short for Grand Sport. The ultimate Buick came at the end of the decade with the 1970 GSX Stage 1 455.

Today, muscle car enthusiasts worldwide recognize how fast those Buick GSX muscle cars were and remain today. The main trouble is, production for 1970 totaled a miniscule 678 units, divided between 491 in Saturn Yellow and 187 in Apollo White.

Ray Witt of Dumas, Texas has owned three of the GSX super cars. Although he appreciates all muscle cars, Buicks are his favorites. He has done 16 muscle car restorations, including a 1970 Pontiac Trans Am, a 1969 Opal GT, a 1953 Buick Roadmaster "woodie" station wagon, three GSX Stage 1s, and the rest Buick GS models.

A used car dealer today, Ray sold out his Chevrolet, Pontiac, and Buick dealership 13 years ago. He claims to have been "raised on Buicks." Like most Buick owners I have met, Ray is very opinionated on the GS and GSX models. When I mentioned that Buick made the GSX in 1971 and 1972, Ray made sure I realized the 1970 was the "only true, full package."

The 1970 GSX is one of those special cars that come along once in a long, long time. The second year saw dilution. Ray says, "In 1971 or 1972 you could order any piece of the package you wanted, such as stripes."

Basically, the 1971 and 1972 GSX suffered from decreased horsepower and torque figures and, overall, the GSX was a trim package.

For 1970, the GSX was the full meal deal. The one caveat to single-mindedness was the choice to two different engines. The base engine was the standard 455. There just wasn't anything very standard about a big block with 510 lb-ft of torque. Interestingly, the base 455 matched the 455 Stage 1 in torque. Horsepower differed by a slim margin of 10 – 350 versus 360. Aficionados of the GSX are quick to point out the true horsepower easily topped 400 for both the base 455 and the Stage 1.

What did the Stage 1 bring to the table? First was the name itself. Stage 1 was an obvious reference to drag racing, where diggers denoted an increase in power in "stages." Buick wisely applied the name to their GSX. No doubt the 455 was right at home on the strip.

Ray explains, "The compression was the same and the block and heads were identical except they cut the valves larger. The Stage 1 has a different curved distributor, a different camshaft and different jets in the Rochester carburetor."

According to Ray, the jetting in the four-barrel carburetor was the same from the standard 455 to the Stage 1 455 when backed by a 4-speed manual transmission.

Each GSX came with "billboard" tires measuring G60 x 15 – at the time, the largest on any American muscle car. The chromed Rallye wheels measured 15 x 7 and were a special "WG" code. The center cap is a red, white and blue Buick crest.

The eight grand hood-mounted tach redlined at 5,000 rpm. The idea was to put the tachometer in line of sight for the driver.

As might be expected, Buick GSX buyers chose the automatic over the manual, with sales figures of 479 to 199. Ray's GSX has the 4-speed. Since Apollo White production numbers are 187 compared to 491 for Saturn Yellow, his car is very rare with this color and transmission option.

Ray came by this car by default. He's been in the Buick hobby for decades and regularly attends national shows. In the late 1980s, he built a Buick station wagon into a tow rig made to resemble a GSX. In 1990, he towed his Buick racecar to the Buick Nationals with the GSX station wagon. The novelty of the wagon attracted major attention. One of the Buick faithful was

Buick inserted the GSX logo into the middle of the rear spoiler.

so enamored with the wagon, he was still thinking about the vehicle a year later. "He called me up and asked if I still had that GSX wagon. I said yes. I used it for a daily driver."

Ray Witt was amazed when he heard the offer. The man had just bought a 1970 GSX Stage 1, an Apollo White car. He had another GSX that needed "touch-up work." Ray was a Buick dealer at the time and had gained a reputation for restoring and detailing Buicks to world-class standards. The deal was too good almost for Ray to believe or to pass up. The man would trade the 58,000-mile GSX he had just purchased in exchange for the novel GSX station wagon and the touch-up work on the other GSX. He shipped both "X's" to Ray in Dumas, Texas. Meanwhile, Ray traded the man his GSX station wagon. The deal was done.

Ray laughs today at his great deal, but explains the pricing and valuation of the cars was quite a bit different in 1991. The deal was fairly equitable then, but the rarity factor today would definitely dictate a different trade.

The GSX had 58,000 miles and was complete. The one fault was rust on the passenger side front floor pan. The air conditioner had dripped condensate into the cab and initiated rust.

Ray's forte is restoration. He explains, "I love to restore."

Starting with such an original, Ray built a masterpiece. At the GSX Reunion in Ohio, out of 27 show cars in concourse judging, Ray had the highest score – 396 out of a possible 400. The closest GSX to him was "three or four points" behind. In total, the Reunion had an astounding 97 GSX cars there, or almost one out of every six cars built.

When Ray took the body off the frame, he found an incredibly original GSX. Matching numbers could be the theme of this build. The heads, intake, carburetor, distributor, alternator, starter, even the air conditioning compressor matched, number-wise and in date codes. Starting with such a good car made the restoration much simpler.

Ray says, "I mean, all I did was send parts off, have them rebuilt, and whatnot. The only thing I tracked down was some original A/C hoses with the right date codes."

Air-conditioning hoses on what one source lists as the hottest mid-sized muscle car ever seems quite odd, as A/C is a power-robbing accessory.

Ray is being overly modest with his assessment of the difficulty of the restoration. He takes his time and does restorations the OEM way. He plated the bolts, for example, to factory. Ray restored this car inch by inch. The 396 points out of 400 attest to his high standards.

The restored bucket seats felt and looked like brand new.

The GS logo – not GSX – appeared on the door panels.

NEXT-GENERATION COLLECTOR CARS

TEXT & PHOTOS BY BARRY KLUCZYK

12 CARS TO POWER THE NEXT WAVE OF THE HOBBY

Confession time. The author of this story wasn't speed-shifting a Chevelle SS 396 on Woodward Avenue in 1969. I was born that year.

Indeed, there are thousands of muscle car enthusiasts in their 30s and 40s who don't have first-hand experience of Detroit's glory days. They're from the next generation – typically referred to as Generation X – and while their enthusiasm for muscle cars is strong, they weren't the cars that demographic group grew up with.

As a card-carrying member of Generation X, I admit my affection for 5.0-liter Mustangs of the late 1980s is as strong as my affinity for an original Boss 302. And coming of age when the prices on muscle cars skyrocketed means my chances of owning a Boss 302 (a 1969 model in Bright Yellow, please) are in parallel with my odds of winning the lottery. In fact, there's an entire story to be written on the future of muscle car ownership, as affluent Baby Boomers drove up the prices to sometimes absurd levels and effectively eliminated the next generation from participating, but that's a topic for a different time.

So, I'm one of those guys who love muscle cars, but didn't grow up with them in those formative high-school years; and lets face it, those adolescent years are where most of our automotive passions were created. We Gen Xers didn't have Barracudas and Fairlanes in the high-school parking lot. We had Omnis and Fairmonts. So cars like the Buick Grand National and those ubiquitous 5.0-liter

Mustangs resonated strongly, because they were dramatically more dynamic than the four-banger front-drivers that permeated our lives.

And because Gen Xers didn't know first-hand the visceral thrill of a high-compression LS6 accelerating between stoplights, we didn't know what we were missing. The Trans Am sliding around in *Smokey and the Bandit* sure looked cool, even if the soundtrack was dubbed with a NASCAR stock car, and the production Trans Ams had only 220 horsepower.

So, while I'll say traditional muscle cars will always appeal to me and my generation, I'll admit, too, that we were influenced by the era we grew up in. And while the Baby Boomers may look down on cars from the late Seventies and early Eighties, a red-blooded car enthusiast in his 30s or 40s secretly longs to own a black 1987 Monte Carlo SS, even if it can't run 12s.

Not surprisingly, as Gen Xers grow older, they're starting to seek out the cars of their youth and they're forming the foundation for the next generation of collector cars. Many of the classic muscle cars weren't even 20 years old when the first wave of collector mania started, with the real push coming about 25-30 years after they were built. The cars from the late Seventies through late Eighties are hitting those mile markers now, with Gen Xers approaching their peak earning years. We've compiled a list of the cars we believe have the most collector potential – those with the greatest chance to increase significantly in value.

Like traditional muscle cars, those with low production numbers, a proper paper trail and original equipment are valued greater. Low mileage counts, too, as much for appearance as collector value. There simply aren't many restoration parts for cars of this era, and low-mileage originals are the least likely to have needs that aren't always easy to meet.

It's not likely that a Buick GNX will set the collector world on fire like a 1971 Hemi 'Cuda convertible, but the cars of Generation X offer an entry into the collector market that has all but priced them out with classic muscle cars.

Time will tell.

1987-93 Mustang LX 5.0 "Notchback"

Think about this for a moment. The Fox-body Mustang that was the foundation of the influential 5.0-liter industry was introduced in 1979, only 15 years after the original Mustang debuted. Those 15 previous years saw three significant body style changes and ran the gamut from the Boss 429 and Shelbys to the Mustang II. The Fox body Mustang lasted 15 model years by itself and lent more than a little DNA to the SN95 generation from 1994-2004. That's a heck of a production legacy.

There are seemingly dozens of standard- and special-edition Fox Mustangs, from the 1982 GT model that launched the iconic "5.0" badges to the 1993 Cobras, but it is the base-model LX 5.0 and the formal (and lighter weight) "notchback" body style that epitomized the 5.0-liter Mustang movement. Its low-frills/high-thrills ratio reenergized the performance industry and immersed a new generation into drag racing and working on its own cars.

And while at one time the streets and staging lanes used to be thick with 5.0-liter "notches," their supply is diminishing – especially the virgin examples. The heavier GT models were made in far greater numbers, and it's almost impossible to find a 5.0-liter Mustang that hasn't had at least some modifications made to it. So an unmolested, well-kept 5.0-liter notchback is a rare find and is likely to be worth more in the future. Rust in the door bottoms and trunk lid is common, as are seats that show wear. Common maladies include door lock actuators that fail, a console ash tray lid that refuses to close and, like most Fords of the era, radio lights that burn out.

If you really want to sell the car quickly down the road – and get the most for it – spend the time to seek out one with a five-speed transmission. Automatics and 5.0-liters are not a popular combination, and if you prefer an automatic car, check whether the transmission has been rebuilt. The AOD four-speeds in those cars come in two versions: has been rebuilt or needs to be rebuilt.

1983-88 Chevrolet Monte Carlo SS/Aerocoupe

Production cars remained pretty brick-like in appearance until the introduction of the 1983 Ford Thunderbird, which ushered in the modern age of aerodynamically-influenced styling that is largely still with us today. It was a sleek car that cut through the wind like a bullet, especially on NASCAR's fast ovals. In contrast, GM's intermediate coupes cut through the atmosphere like the box the bullets came in.

Chevrolet quickly responded to the "aero" T-birds with a sloped fascia on the blunt nose of the Monte Carlo. It was the inception of the Monte Carlo SS production model, which debuted in 1983 – albeit with a weak, 169hp 305 engine. The sleek styling helped a bit on the racetrack, but launched a very popular street car that has the makings of one of the few true collector cars from the 1980s.

The Monte Carlos SS is an icon of its era, looking no better than in black. Curiously, black wasn't originally an SS color. White and blue were the only choices in 1983 and 1984, with 1984 models introducing the perkier, 180hp 305 that would last the duration of the model's production. Black was added in 1985. The Monte Carlo SS was popular from the get-go, with more than 4,700 sold in 1983 and a huge jump to more than 24,000 sales in 1985. More than 41,000 were sold in 1986, the model's peak year.

While the styling of the Monte Carlo SS was a hit, it was still missing something on the racetrack. The sharp, vertical cut-off behind the C-pillar and long rear deck caused airflow turbulence at high speed, including unwanted lift. It just wasn't competitive with the T-bird. The solution came in the form of a sloping, fastback-style rear window that effectively replaced the rear deck lid, giving the car greater stability and about a 5-mph boost in top speed. A scant 200 production examples were built in 1986, and 6,052 were built in 1987.

All Monte Carlo SSs suffer from typically-GM quality of the day, which means thin lacquer paint that didn't hold up well, easily worn interiors (including door pulls that are notoriously prone to breaking) and valve seals that wear out around the 60,000-mile mark, causing that characteristic blue-smoke puff on cold starts. The best hedge against those problems is finding a low-mile, unmodified example. Some buyers will try to persuade you their 350 engine swap makes the car more powerful and, therefore, more desirable, but the collector status of Monte Carlo SS and Aerocoupe models lie in their originality.

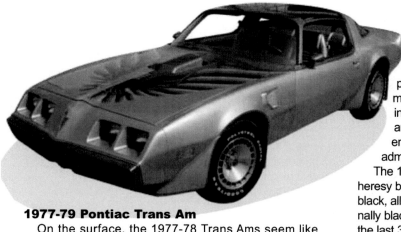

1977-79 Pontiac Trans Am

On the surface, the 1977-78 Trans Ams seem like no-brainers for our list. They're the *Smokey and the Bandit*-styled cars and have the equivalent cultural resonance as orange 1969 Dodge Chargers with "01" painted on the doors. So it seems strange that we're also including the 1979 models on our list, because they had the admittedly less-desirable "split headlight" front-end styling. But here's the thing: 1979 represented the last year for the true Pontiac V-8 in the Trans Am, and those last-year cars have come to be quite collectable to Pontiac purists, especially the 10th anniversary models.

There's a caveat to the 1979 models' desirability, however,

and it all depends on the lettering on the car's shaker-style hood scoop. If it reads "T/A 6.6," the car is powered by a Pontiac 400 and backed by a four-speed manual transmission. If it reads "6.6 Litre," you're looking at a car saddled with an Olds-sourced 403 engine and slushbox trans. To be perfectly honest, the Olds engine was just as stout as the Pontiac 400 and was admirably smooth, but it just wasn't a Pontiac mill.

The 1977 and 1978 models get away with their underhood heresy because of one word: Bandit. If it's a 1977 or 1978 and black, all is forgiven. And if it is a 1977 or 1978 and not originally black, there a good chance the color was changed during the last 30 years, so check the trim tag carefully. Originality is always worth more.

As for those 1979 10th anniversary models, only 1,817 of the 7,500 built were equipped with the Pontiac 400 engine/four-speed combination, making them very desirable.

1986-87 Buick Grand National/ 1987 Buick GNX

Turbo Buicks had been around since the late 1970s, but the addition of an intercooler to the 3.8L V-6 in 1986 was the catalyst that transformed a merely good engine into a great one in the Buick Grand National. It was immediately elevated from respected performer to factory hot rod icon. The intercooler pushed output from 1985's rating of 200 horsepower to 235 – with 330 lb-ft of torque. Horsepower increased to 245 in 1987.

Out of the box, the Grand National could hit 60 mph in about 5 seconds flat and, if the driver was good, clip the quarter-mile in about 13.9 seconds. Nothing – and we mean *nothing* – was running 13s from the factory in those days. Not surprisingly, it was a strong seller, with more than 5,500 sold in 1986 and nearly 21,000 sold in 1987.

In a perfect, go-out-on-a-high-note performance, Buick commemorated the end of the G-body platform and the Grand National model with the sinister-looking, 276-horsepower GNX. Only 547 were built, and they became instant collector items and remain valuable holdovers from the 1980s.

Like the popular muscle cars of the 1960s, many Grand National owners were quick to modify their car, so low-mileage and unmodified examples are getting more scarce. Also, the original lacquer paint jobs were notoriously thin and haven't stood up well over the years – even on otherwise well-preserved examples. Excellent, original cars are out there, but they'll cost you. And the still-in-the-wrapper GNXs are pushing six figures.

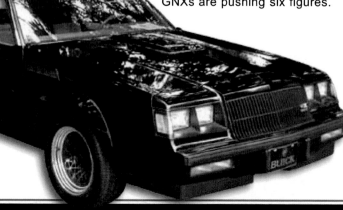

1983-84 Hurst/Olds

Let's be clear. The 1983-84 Hurst/Olds are not fast cars. Their small-block V-8s deliver a satisfying feel of torque, and they're great cruisers, but they're not about to embarrass any muscle car-era W-30 cars between stoplights. And that's just fine.

The appeal of the 1983-84 Hurst/Olds models is their G-body styling, which was the last of GM's traditional body-on-frame rear-drive intermediates, and their special-edition styling cues. Simply put, they were great looking cars that appealed to two generations – the original muscle car jockeys and the Gen X enthusiasts who grew up after them.

The 1983 H/O was designed to commemorate the 15th anniversary of the original, 1968 model. Only 3,001 examples were built (201 sold in Canada), all of them black with a silver lower body and red dividing stripe. Each came off Olds' assembly line in Lansing, Michigan and was shipped about 45 miles away to secondary manufacturer Cars and Concepts for the conversion. The Hurst Olds returned in 1984 with a silver-over-black paint scheme that was essentially a reversal of the first-year model. The only real product difference was the change to a larger, 8.5-inch rear axle. Production increased to 3,500 units.

Performance-wise, every Hurst Olds packed a four-barrel-fed, 180hp 307ci engine, a Hydra-Matic 200-4R overdrive transmission and a 3.73 rear axle. Along with its 180 horses was a solid 245 lb-ft of torque. It was a combination good for 16-second quarter-miles and 0-60 sprints of about 9 seconds.

1976-78 Ford Mustang II Cobra/1978 Mustang King Cobra

After the halcyon days of the Mustang's first generation, storm clouds massed with the introduction of the Pinto-based Mustang II in 1974. Only four short years after a customer could walk into a Ford showroom and pick a Boss 429, Boss 302 or Cobra Jet-equipped model, the 1974 Mustang wasn't even offered with a V-8 (except in Mexico). The public was not thrilled. Nor did they clamor for the second-generation car like they did the first.

Something had to be done, and in the finest tradition of the Seventies, that "something" was tape stripes. With the assistance from GTO marketing guru Jim Wangers' company, the Cobra II was introduced in 1976. It was offered in V-6 and V-8 models, so outright performance wasn't its forte, but a healthy aftermarket helped enthusiasts squeeze a little more juice from their lackluster engines. With no pretensions that it was a high-performance car, the Cobra II was an attractive package that was made more popular by its frequent placement on *Charlie's Angels*. Thousands were sold during its three-year run.

And while the Cobra II was popular with its period graphics package, the 1978-only King Cobra took the concept to the extreme, with a huge, expressive hood graphic, a large front air dam and other unique appointments – including a hood scoop graphic that glimpsed the future: "5.0." There were 4,318 King Cobras sold.

Mustang IIs have always struggled for respect, but thanks to Gen X enthusiasts who embrace them, the Cobra IIs and King Cobras are gaining increasing favor among collectors.

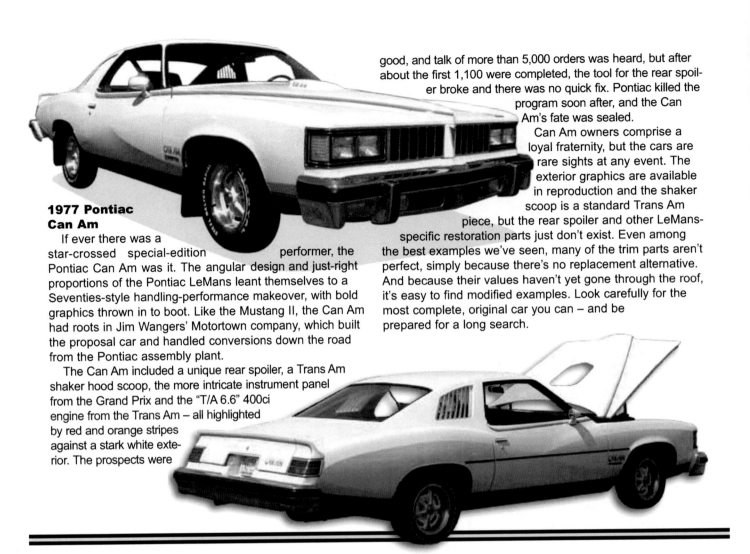

1977 Pontiac Can Am

If ever there was a star-crossed special-edition performer, the Pontiac Can Am was it. The angular design and just-right proportions of the Pontiac LeMans leant themselves to a Seventies-style handling-performance makeover, with bold graphics thrown in to boot. Like the Mustang II, the Can Am had roots in Jim Wangers' Motortown company, which built the proposal car and handled conversions down the road from the Pontiac assembly plant.

The Can Am included a unique rear spoiler, a Trans Am shaker hood scoop, the more intricate instrument panel from the Grand Prix and the "T/A 6.6" 400ci engine from the Trans Am – all highlighted by red and orange stripes against a stark white exterior. The prospects were good, and talk of more than 5,000 orders was heard, but after about the first 1,100 were completed, the tool for the rear spoiler broke and there was no quick fix. Pontiac killed the program soon after, and the Can Am's fate was sealed.

Can Am owners comprise a loyal fraternity, but the cars are rare sights at any event. The exterior graphics are available in reproduction and the shaker scoop is a standard Trans Am piece, but the rear spoiler and other LeMans-specific restoration parts just don't exist. Even among the best examples we've seen, many of the trim parts aren't perfect, simply because there's no replacement alternative. And because their values haven't yet gone through the roof, it's easy to find modified examples. Look carefully for the most complete, original car you can – and be prepared for a long search.

1978-81 Chevrolet Camaro Z28

The late Seventies and early Eighties were all about the Camaro. Chevrolet sold more than 282,000 Camaros in 1979, including about 50,000 Z28s (more than 54,000 Zs were sold in 1978). Those production numbers were never topped again.

What's surprising about the Camaro's popularity in that era was the fact the second-generation platform was already quite long in the tooth. It was introduced in 1970, but continual styling refinements turned out a great looking car when sleek urethane front and rear fascias were introduced in 1978.

And while there were tens of thousands of Z28s built during those four influential model years, few remain untouched. Like the new, fifth-generation Camaros, they were modified and personalized by owners moments after delivery. They were turned into street machines, bracket racers and more, before becoming the budget hot rods for a generation of high-school throttle jockeys. Plain and simple, most of the cars were beaten to death. Pristine examples are out there and many restoration parts are available – and the prices are only going up with each passing

1976-80 Dodge Aspen R/T/ Plymouth Volaré Road Runner

OK, Mopar fans, here's your lone entry on our list – mostly because Chrysler was switching to their front-drive era about the time Gen Xers were noticing cars.

Like the Mustang II, the Dodge Aspen and Plymouth Volaré were shadows of the performance cars they replaced, but it was the Seventies after all, so sporty models with decals and performance monikers were all but required by law. Again, they were rivals for Hemis or Six-Pack cars offered at the start of the decade, but the Aspen R/T and Volaré Road Runner offered stout 360 and 318 engine options that delivered strong torque and respectable performance. Special "Kit Car" models

in 1978 added a greater dimension of exclusivity, and they're exceptionally rare today – especially in good condition.

Apart from the special body kits on the Kit Car examples, there isn't much to distinguish the R/T and Road Runner models from their plain-Jane cousins, apart from graphics, some blacked-out trim and, on some models, rear quarter window slats. Here's the good news – apart from some of those crazy collectors who believe all Mopars worth their weight in gold, these cars are cheap! The trick is finding one that won't cost more than it's worth to shine up.

1975-76 Buick Indy Pace Car Replica/"Free Spirit"

The rare and seldom-seen Buick Indy pace car replicas of 1975 and 1976 epitomize the graphics-heavy approach to specialty cars in the years after the muscle car era.

Starting in the mid-1970s and lasting through the late 1980s, Buick was a force in open-wheel racing, with its very successful V-6 turbo program. Supplying the pace cars for the Indianapolis 500 for two consecutive years was a direct result of its involvement. In those days, the cars required considerable modifications to handle the high-speed duties on the track, but the promotional models offered for sale to the public were mostly tape-stripe spe-

cials. That was the case with the Buicks, although in addition to their pace car references, they were touted as "Free Spirit" editions to mirror Buick's primary marketing campaign.

Despite different color schemes, graphics and exterior styling, both the 1975 and 1976 cars had Hurst Hatch "T-tops." The 1975 model was V-8-powered, while the 1976 had a V-6 to align with the V-6 engine that powered the real pace car that year. These cars are very difficult to find and excellent-condition examples only more so, but they attract attention, and you're bound to be the only enthusiast at the show – or in the county or state, for that matter – with one.

1985-90 Chevrolet Camaro IROC-Z

Third-generation Camaros suffer from a collective identity problem. They were very popular in the 1980s, but are often associated with, shall we say, less-than-fashionable demographics. The image of teased-hair bleach-blonde girls and mullet-styled guys cruising with the T-top panels removed really had nothing to do with the inherent capabilities of the cars.

IROC models, of course, were named for the racing series that used Camaros. The street-going versions were higher-performing models than the Z28s and, soon, their popularity would push the Z28 into the dark. They cornered and stopped better than the Mustangs of the day, and when equipped with the optional 350 engine (automatic trans only, unfortunately), they were competitive between stoplights.

The IROC was a cultural phenomenon. Mention the name to anyone who grew up in the Eighties, and even if they don't know a lug nut from a steering wheel, they know the car – for better or worse. Prices are still reasonable, but they're climbing. The biggest problem is the deficit of restoration parts, so your best bet is finding the most original, lowest-mileage example you can.

1991 GMC Syclone/1992-93 GMC Typhoon

The GMC Syclone was the crazy kind of vehicle the conservative General Motors simply wasn't known for producing. It was a compact pickup with a turbocharged 4.3-liter V-6 and all-wheel drive that sucked the doors off just about anything it encountered, including a Ferrari in an infamous *Car and Driver* story. It was offered only in sinister black, with a unique lower body kit. It was bold, brash and very un-GM. Unfortunately, it was a two-seat truck and you couldn't tow with it, so few people bought it strictly for its hair-raising performance – only 1,995 to be exact.

When it was clear the brilliant Syclone wasn't succeeding, GMC came at the idea from a different angle and applied the Syclone's styling and drivetrain, along with some new exterior colors, to the Jimmy compact SUV and dubbed it the Typhoon. It was more successful than the Syclone, selling nearly 4,700

examples during its two-year run.

Nearly 20 years later, these trucks are revered by a cult-like legion of enthusiasts. Buy one and you're in the club, but be wary of excessive mods and non-original engines. The 4.3-liter foundation didn't cotton to mods like the Buick 3.8-liter turbo engine, so more than a few were blown up or severely weakened.

1974 Dodge Dart
A CLASSIC MUSCLE CAR FOR UNDER $10K

Text by Joe Babiasz, photos by Ryan Merrill

The early 1970s are regarded as the performance peak for factory muscle cars; however, by the mid-Seventies, performance cars were nearly non-existent. Federal emissions guidelines had put a stake in the heart of almost all muscle cars, and their replacements became crude caricatures of a glorious past. Body stripes, phony scoops, and special wheels replaced tire-smoking power. Regulations pushed compression ratios lower, and leaner fuel mixtures resulted in reduced horsepower. Combined with the increased vehicle weight necessary to meet five-mph

bumper crash tests, and what buyers were left with wasn't very appealing. However, Chrysler still had a few tricks up its sleeve, and pulled the proverbial rabbit out of their hat. Enter the 1974 Dodge Dart.

The Dart was available in two distinctive body platforms. The 108-inch wheelbase Dart Sport and Sport 360 were essentially Dodge's version of the pillared two-door Plymouth Duster. The longer 111-inch wheelbase Dart and Dart Custom were available only as four-door sedans, and were aimed at families. The stylish Dart Swinger and Swinger Special also rode on a

111-inch wheelbase, and were the only true two-door hardtops in the Dart line.

Exterior changes from 1973 were kept to a minimum. All models received a redesigned rear bumper able to withstand 1974's federally mandated, five-mph rear bumper crash test. Taillights on the Dart, Dart Custom, and Dart Swinger were enlarged and repositioned from the rear bumper to the tail panel just above the bumper. Ten new exterior colors were added for a total of 16.

Inside, little changed. Bench seats were standard, with bucket seats available as an option that required

The Dart Sport 360 was the ultimate low-price performance car. Standard equipment included the four-barrel, 360 cubic-inch V-8, front anti-sway bar, rally suspension, dual exhausts, and special body stripes.

community, the Hang 10 checked off every box when it came to illustrating that image. Standard equipment included orange shag carpeting, multi-colored seat and door pad inserts, fold-down rear seats, and a red and white side stripe with the image of a surfer riding a wave at the back end of the stripe. A Hang 10 logo was placed on the hood and decklid. The only exterior color was eggshell white. Customers had a slew of options to choose from including racing mirrors, rally wheels, and either a half or full vinyl top. Engine options ranged from the Slant Six to the 360 cubic-inch V-8.

Another mid-year introduction was the Dart SE (Special Edition). Aimed at providing a more luxurious small car, the SE featured velour high back bucket seats, carpeted door panels, a woodgrain instrument panel, and deluxe wheel covers. A vinyl roof and special hood ornament were also standard. The only transmission available was Chrysler's dependable TorqueFlite.

The year 1974 was successful for the Dart. With a wide range of engines and body styles, buyers kept coming back for more. For the performance minded, the Dart was quick enough— but it was the simple styling, low price, and numerous options that made it a success.

the customer to order the center console. A new "Unibelt" seat belt system replaced the difficult-to-use, separate lap and shoulder belt. An extra cost, manually operated sunroof was available on the Dart Sport, Dart 360 Sport, and Swinger models. To overcome previous complaints about keeping the car cooled, the air conditioning system had its capacity increased.

Chrysler's Slant Six and 318 V-8 engines were carried over from 1973. The 340 cubic-inch engine was replaced by a more emissions-friendly 360 cubic-inch V-8. Rated at 245 horsepower, the 360 provided brisk

performance in the lightweight Dart while using regular gas.

The Dart Sport 360 was the ultimate low-price performance car. Standard equipment included the four-barrel, 360 cubic-inch V-8, front anti-sway bar, rally suspension, dual exhausts, and special body stripes. Front disc brakes were standard on the Sport 360, as well as on all V-8 equipped Darts. Transmission choi-ces included a three-speed manual, four-speed manual, and TorqueFlite automatic.

Mid-year, the Hang 10 model was introduced. Designed to reflect the image of the laid-back surfing

SPECIFICATIONS

Number built – 263,467 (no Dart four-door sedan numbers)

Construction – Unibody

Engines – 198 cubic-inch Slant Six, 225 cubic-inch Slant Six, 318 cubic-inch V-8, 360 cubic-inch V-8

Power/Torque – 198 cubic-inch Slant Six, 95 horsepower, 145 lb-ft torque, 225 cubic-inch Slant Six, 105 horsepower, 180 lb-ft torque, 318 cubic-inch V-8, 150 horsepower, 255 lb-ft torque, 360 cubic-inch V-8, 245 horsepower, 320 lb-ft torque

Transmissions – Three-speed manual, four-speed manual, three-speed automatic

Suspension front – Independent, lateral, non-parallel control arms with torsion bars

Suspension rear – Longitudinal leaf springs with live axle

Steering – Re-circulating ball

Brakes – Four-wheel drum (six-cylinder), front disc, rear drum (V-8)

Length/width/height – 201.7/69.6/54.1 inches

Wheelbase – 111 inches

Weight – 3,330 lbs.

0-60 mph/quarter mile – 9.6 seconds, 16.8 seconds at 80 mph (*Motor Trend,* April 1974 testing a Dodge 318 cubic-inch V-8)

Top speed – N/A

MPG – 13 - 17 mpg est.

Price – MSRP - $3,518 (Dart Swinger hardtop); Today - $3,600 - $8,950

Photos courtesy of NAHC

NEW DART SPORT "HANG TEN"

DART SPORT CONVERTRIPLE '74.

FUEL FOR THOUGHT

- Electronic ignition was standard
- 27% of coupe buyers were under 25
- Performance 3.55:1 axle ratio available
- Four-speed not available with six-cylinder

ENGINE

Both the Slant Sixes and the V-8s are extremely dependable. The 360 cubic-inch V-8 came with an oil windage tray, shot-peened crankshaft, and heavy-duty rod and main bearings. An abundance of aftermarket parts are available to improve performance.

HANDLING

Handling was typical for its time. While the V-8 added horsepower, it also added weight to the front end. Cornering was adequate at best. The standard front disc brakes (V-8 cars) gave good stopping power.

STRONG POINTS

• Low purchase price

• Parts readily available

• Excellent styling

WEAK POINTS

• Typical rust issues

• Low-compression engine

• Limited appreciation

WHAT TO PAY

1974 DODGE DART SWINGER

- MSRP – $3,518
- Low – $3,600
- Average – $5,575
- High – $8,950

Based on prices from NADA.

INSURANCE COST

Insurance cost is $143/year for a $5,575 1974 Dodge Dart Swinger. This is based on 3,000 miles per year of pleasure driving.

Based on a quote from Heacock Classic Car Insurance www.heacockclassic.com

PARTS PRICES

- Front floor pan $195.00
- Quarter panel $329.00
- Brake rotor $59.00
- Dash Bezel $250.00
- Fuel Tank $289.00
- Engine wiring harness $189.00

Based on information from National Mo-Parts Inc. 705-426-2993 www.nationalmoparts.com

VEHICLE CATEGORY

The 1974 Dart is an entry-level, "driver" vehicle. Owners enjoy using them on a regular basis.

BOOKS

- *Dodge Dart 1960-76* **by R.M. Clarke**
- *Chrysler Performance Upgrades* **by Frank Adkins**
- *Dodge Dart and Plymouth Duster (Muscle Car Color History)* **by Steve Statham**

WEBSITES

www.allpar.com
www.mopartopsites.com
www.hangtenregistry.com
www.chryslerclub.org

ALTERNATIVE

1974 AMC Javelin

Number built – 2,282

0-60/quarter-mile – 11.2 seconds, 17.2 seconds at 83 mph (304 cubic-inch V-8)

Top speed – 105 mph est.

Price – MSRP - $3,093; Today – $3,675 - $12,850

ALTERNATIVE

1974 Pontiac GTO

Number built – 5,335

0-60/quarter-mile – 9.4 seconds, 16.5 seconds at 84 mph

Top speed – 109 mph est.

Price – MSRP - $2,910; Today – $6,250 - $18,900

REVIEW

The Dart was designed to be a low-priced family and/or performance car. It did little exceptionally well, but in general was reliable and dependable. The Sport 360 was an exciting car for 1974. Performance was among the best of any domestic vehicle. It held its own without the visual bells and whistles many other so-called muscle cars had.

No-Frills Muscle Cobra

1969 *Fairlane 500* *Cobra*

Text and images by Jerry Heasley

One of the more perplexing muscle cars of the sizzling Sixties was the 1969 Cobra. Or was that the Fairlane Cobra? Or, more to the point, was this mid-sized Ford a Fairlane 500 Cobra? Some people mistakenly apply the term Torino Cobra.

The original Cobra was Carroll Shelby's two-seat, aluminum-bodied roadster, first with a small block V-8 (260 and a 289), followed by perhaps the most awesome muscle car of all time, the infamous 427 Cobra. The small block Cobra decimated the Corvette in domestic road racing and beat Ferrari internationally to win the world champion-ship of makes for GT cars. The big block could go from 0 to 60 mph in less than four seconds and proved invincible in its SCCA road racing class.

At the end of the 1967 model year, when Carroll's company, Shelby-American, quit making their 2200-pound sports car, Ford attached the nameplate to the 1968 Shelby Mustang. The new GT350s and GT500s were the new Cobras. There was no profit to letting such a storied nameplate go to waste. No other badge had quite so much charisma in the United States as the Cobra.

Where else could Ford make use of the Cobra badge?

They had no two-seater sports car. In 1969, the Shelby Mustang became the GT series. Ford attached the Cobra name to a hot version of the Fairlane, powered by the 428 Cobra Jet big-block.

In seven model years, the Cobra had moved from a tiny roadster that was mostly a racecar, to a pony car, and finally to a mid-sized Ford muscle car.

The downside was the tremendous legacy that fell upon a no-frills, mid-sized Ford with the gas-sipping heritage of the Fairlane. In this role, Ford Division built the Cobra to take on the no-frills muscle cars springing up in Detroit. The original "econo-muscle car," as the magazines dubbed this new breed, was Plymouth's 1968 Road Runner, based off the Belvedere/Satellite. Dodge's version was the Super Bee, based off the mid-sized Coronet.

Mother Mopar caught the rest of Detroit off-guard in 1968. The Big Three made money by selling options, which could quickly run the price of a muscle car over and above the budget of the young buyers. Dodge and Plymouth got wise. They built the Road Runner and Super Bee into an inexpensive mid-sized coupe or sedan. Mopar's target was a mid-14-second quarter-mile mauler for less than $3,000. Cost-adding options, such as the 440 Six Pack or the dual quad Hemi, were mainly performance, or just what the American youth wanted.

For the Cobra, Ford Division started with the Fairlane 500. There was an upscale Torino and Torino GT in the same mid-sized body style. The Fairlane 500 started with a lower base price and fit the formula of an economy muscle car. They replaced Fairlane badges with Cobra. From there, Ford went for the jugular by making the 428 Cobra Jet big block the standard engine, besting the base 383 in the Road Runner and Super Bee by 45 cubic inches. The horsepower figures for the 383 and the 428 CJ were the same, at 335. However, the 428 CJ pulled more like 400 horsepower. Ford slid the horsepower numbers down to give their 428 CJ an edge in the Super Stock drag racing classes.

Ford adorned the front fenders of early Cobras with Cobra cartoon style decals. Later, they switched to more serious die cast badges, as seen on this 1969 Cobra.

Why the Cobra did not sell well is anybody's guess. My guess is the Road Runner was new and cheap and really caught on. Cobra came a year later to the party. The Cobra badge was a little confusing on a mid-sized mauler. The Cobra, in my opinion, fit a much sportier model. The Cobra heritage was a flashy two-seat roadster.

Bob restored the engine to stock, including the original compressor for air conditioning. This 428 Cobra Jet is a CJ-R, for ram air. This is the R-code, denoted by the fifth digit of the VIN. The base engine was the Q-code, or non-ram air 428 CJ. Both rated 335 horsepower. Ford also offered the 428 Super Cobra Jet, with or without ram air. In either case, you got the Drag Pack components, consisting of 3.91:1 or 4.30:1 rear axle, external oil cooler and Le Mans rods.

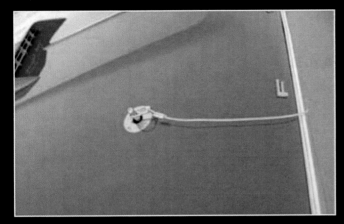

(One can only imagine the confusion if Chevrolet ended Corvette production and attached the badge to a low-end Chevelle with a big engine.)

First year Road Runner sales shot through the proverbial roof. Product planners guessed a run of 2,000, but 1968 model year production topped an incredible 45,000 units. The Fairlane Cobra could not muster a third of this total in its first model year, 1969.

Still, the Ford's new Cobra was a formidable car. Despite the Fairlane heritage of economy, the 1969 Sportsroof, seen here, was pure performance, starting with a "Sportsroof" body style with a radical rear roofline. The mid-sized Fairlane was Ford's NASCAR entry, and

designers took into account aerodynamics. Blacking out the trim and inserting Cobra badges on the Sportsroof created a great looking muscle car fitted with the right pieces for the muscle car wars.

The 4-speed was standard, as was a stout nine-inch rear end. The Drag Pack added an external oil cooler, 3.91:1 or 4.30:1 gears in a Traction-Lok differential, plus stouter engine internals, including Le Mans connecting rods for durability on the drag strip.

The Cobra was the muscle machine Ford needed to compete with the Chevelle SS 396, Road Runner, Super Bee, 4-4-2, GTO, and Buick Grand Sport. With the Cobra, buyers received a muscle car turnkey-ready to take on

Bench seats have gone the way of the dodo bird on today's cars. Among the muscle car cognoscenti, plain bench seats add to the no-nonsense character of a 1960s big block American mid-sized coupe or sedan.

The interior utilized four pods for circular gauges. This Cobra did not come with an in-dash tachometer. This could have been a cost-saving measure. For drag racing, most diggers added their own tach, anyway.

Hook lock pins and wires are are de rigueur on a classic muscle car. Luckily, the Cobra had them. *(far left)*

The hood scoop shares looks with the hood scoop on the 1969 Mach 1. However, the Mach 1's scoop was non-functional. This channels outside air to the top of the engine via a flapper assembly and seal. *(left)*

From the rear, the Sportsroof body style gave the fastback Fairlane a very different look from the rest of the Ford lineup. *(right)*

What's in a name? Shelby's original Cobra topped $6,000 with a small block in the early 1960s. In the late 1960s, the base price on this Cobra was a hundred dollars or so over three grand, or about half the cost of a new Cobra in 1963. Going down in price did not help the prestige of the Cobra nameplate. The Cobra name did not fit the economy muscle car theme. *(below)*

1969 Cobra

Model*	Series	Body Code**
63B	Fairlane 500	46 (Sportsroof with bench seat)
63E	Fairlane 500	46 (Sportsroof with bucket seats)
65A	Fairlane 500	45 (Formal hardtop with bench seats)
65E	Fairlane 500	45 (Formal hardtop with bucket seats)

* Body code, as revealed on the trim tag.
** Body code as revealed in the third and fourth digits of the VIN.

As the chart shows, Ford built the 1969 Cobra in the Fairlane 500 series in both the Sportsroof (Ford's marketing name for the fastback) and the formal roof hardtop. Each body style came with either bench or bucket seats. The Torino and Torino GT were slightly upscale in trim and did not fit the economy muscle car theme upon which Ford built the 1969 Cobra. Interestingly enough, the name Fairlane 500 did not appear on the body. "FORD" is spelled out on the leading edge of the hood and on the rear tail light board.

any other mid-sized muscle car out of Detroit.

One of those buyers was a man with the last name of Hatfield from Tulsa, Oklahoma. He titled this Candyapple Red "Sportsroof" on May 1st of 1969. Although we don't know the deal he made, the sticker price was $4,077, delivered to Doenges Brothers Ford, Fifth Ave. at Detr., Tulsa, Oklahoma.

Ten options and accessories pushed the price well above the level of an economy muscle car. Seven of those 10 extras were unnecessary for performance – the C-6 Cruise-O-Matic automatic transmission, Visibility Group, power steering, tinted glass- complete, AM radio, air conditioning, and color-keyed racing mirrors.

Every Cobra came at no extra charge with the 428 Cobra Jet. Collectors refer to this standard engine as the Q-code. One step up was the R-code, seen under the hood of this car. R is short for ram air. The 428 CJ-R Cobra channeled air through the centrally-mounted hood scoop to a flapper assembly on top of the air cleaner. The Drag Pack was optional on either the Q-code or the R-code.

The three performance upgrades on this car were the Traction-Lok differential, F70 x 14 traction tires with raised white letters, and power front disc brakes. Obviously, the original owner could have done much better on price had

he been less luxury-minded. Auto companies still gave the economy muscle car buyer comfort and convenience options and accessories to jack up the price. The set of 3.00:1 gears were better suited for cruising than drag racing, which probably explains checking off air conditioning on the order form.

The first owner kept the car until 1999, or thirty years. The second owner swapped out the automatic for a 4-speed, and by the time the current owner, Bob Fries, bought the vehicle in 2006, the 42,000-mile original wasn't so original anymore. Bob described his purchase as "a car in a box" and "a basket case." Luckily, the parts were all there. Bob owns Century Motor Works, LLC in Tulsa.

"We do mechanical repairs and restoration, mostly," Bob says. He farms out the bodywork and painting. Fries is also an enthusiast and bought this car to restore and keep. At this writing, he is also putting together a 1964 Galaxie with an R-code – that's the dual quad 427.

Bob showed his 1969 Fairlane Cobra at the 2010 Mid-America Ford and Team Shelby Nationals. Bob's goal is to show, cruise and drag race. Currently, he has installed a set of digger 4.30:1 gears "to play with" on the strip. When drag racing season is over, he'll swap back the set of stock 3.00:1 gears for cruising.

The Sportsroof had a fairly radical rear roofline. Ford adored the pillars with three chrome strips.

The dog dish hubcaps certainly fit the economy muscle car theme. They worked great for drag racing, too. The driver simply popped off the caps with a screwdriver or lug wrench and went drag racing. The center crest on the caps is the Fairlane crown.

TIME TO TAKE CHARGE.

THE OPTIMA® CHARGERS FAMILY OF CHARGERS AND MAINTAINERS

BEST-IN-CLASS FEATURES

Digital 1200	Digital 400

Quick Set Selections
Quick and easy selection of charge profiles by battery type.

USB / Maintenance Port
USB and maintenance charging port for easy, off-season battery maintaining.

Integrated Cable Wrap & Storage
Cable wrap body and reusable cord tie design secures cables for easy storage.

Innovative Multi-Use Design
Dual purpose hook and tilt design allows for in-vehicle hanging or angled stand viewing.

Created by the leader in high-performance AGM batteries, the new OPTIMA Chargers family of products are microprocessor-controlled and will enhance the performance of all types of lead-acid vehicle batteries. They are specifically designed to make AGM batteries carry more power and last longer. They even recover deeply discharged batteries that other chargers can't handle. They charge, condition and maintain all types of 12V flooded and AGM batteries. Stop compromising. It's time to take charge and give your battery high-efficiency charging with OPTIMA Chargers. OPTIMA® CHARGERS. The Ultimate Power Source.™

Now available at participating **Retailers** and optimabatteries.com

 Johnson Controls

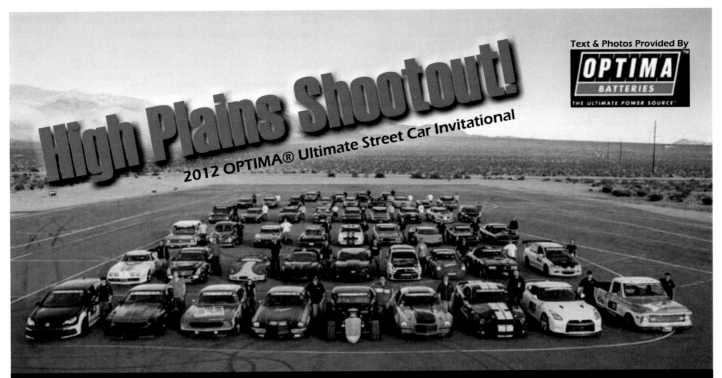

High Plains Shootout!

2012 OPTIMA® Ultimate Street Car Invitational

The fifth annual OPTIMA® Ultimate Street Car Invitational, presented by K&N Filters and Royal Purple, brought in massive crowds with a sold out event, more thrilling moments and record times, ultimately crowning Mark Stielow and his custom 1967 Chevrolet Camaro as the 2012 OPTIMA Ultimate Street Car. It was a year for close competition with the top two participants separated by a single point and a tie for third place overall. Additionally, there was a more diverse showing of vehicles this year with nearly 20 percent of the field falling under the import category.

The OPTIMA Invitational packed the grandstands with non-stop activity, something for everyone in the manufacturer midway, on-the-ground excitement of television personalities (Amanda Salas and Bill Goldberg) filming the miniseries finale of the OPTIMA Ultimate Street Car Invitational broadcast series.

The main race events of the OPTIMA Ultimate Street Car Invitational took place Saturday, November 3, with the BFGoodrich Hot Lap Challenge, Ridetech Autocross Challenge, Wilwood Disc Brakes Speed Stop Challenge, and the Lingenfelter Performance Engineering Performance and Design Challenge. The Detroit Speed and Engineering/JRI Shocks Road Rally occurred following the close of the SEMA Show Friday, November 2.

The Strength of Stielow

With only a point to spare, Mark Stielow, known to some as the 'Godfather of the Pro-Touring movement,' claimed his second OPTIMA Ultimate Street Car Invitational title in four attempts. Stielow scored a total of 83 points, out of a total 110 possible across all events, beating second-place finisher, Brian Hobaugh.

Both Stielow and Hobaugh picked up 10 points each in the Detroit Speed & Engineering/JRI Shocks Road Rally. Stielow saw a 16-12 advantage in the Lingenfelter Performance Design Challenge and a 25-22 edge in the RideTech Autocross. Hobaugh topped Stielow 25-22 in the

BFGoodrich Hot Lap Challenge and 13-10 in the Wilwood Disc Brakes Speed Stop Challenge.

"For a car I just got running four weeks ago, I felt we did better than I dreamed of in the OPTIMA Invitational. I give a lot of the credit to my partners on assembling the car, and a cast of friends that really helped out when the timing was tight. The thing that pushed this car over the top to win was its styling and the street usability of the car," said Stielow. Finally, Stielow acknowledged how much the event has evolved saying, "This event is an incredibly fun yet competitive experience, and the versatility and performance of the vehicles are better than ever."

Mark started auto crossing at the age of 18 in a 1966 MGB, which he purchased for $300. Now Mark, who has built seven magazine quality cars, has been featured in high profile publications such as Car and Driver and Hot Rod and has authored Pro Touring Engineered Performance.

OPTIMA Invitational Automotive Celebrity Integrations

New this year, OPTIMA Batteries welcomed a number of well-known automotive celebrity racers to run in the event exhibition class including NASCAR racer Dylan Kwasniewski, Freightliner racer Mike Ryan and Erik Buell Racing rider Geoff May.

Up-and-coming NASCAR favorite Dylan Kwasniewski set the tone for the day with a pace lap of 1 minute 38 seconds on the OPTIMA Invitational road course, with the next best participant coming in at 1 minute 46 seconds. At 17 years old, Kwasniewski has already been named NASCAR's Next 9, an elite list of top NASCAR prospects. For the past two years he has piloted the No. 03 Rockstar Energy/Royal Purple Ford for Gene Price Motorsports in the NASCAR K&N Pro Series West.

A favorite with spectators was professional race driver and Hollywood stuntman Mike Ryan driving a Freightliner on the road course as part of an exhibition round.

Another first in OPTIMA Invitational history was a battle of two-wheel vs. four-wheel. The exhibition match-up featured Mark Stielow's high-performing 1969 Chevrolet Camaro and a 2013 1190RS Erik Buell Racing (EBR) motorcycle, which was street-prepped and driven by Geoff May. Stielow beat May by one split second, and the thrill of the competition got the crowd to their feet with excitement.

Charitable Elements

Many of the OPTIMA Invitational participants teamed up for a never-been-done-before, heart warming charitable effort. Beginning at the SEMA Show Pro-Touring dinner, Rob McGregor initiated the movement by committing a designated dollar amount to the Wounded Warrior Project for every participant he placed ahead of in the OPTIMA Invitational. The group learned that the cause is near and dear to McGregor's heart as his nephew is currently serving in Afghanistan. Several other participants followed and together OPTIMA Invitational participants raised more than $20,000 for the Wounded Warrior Project over the weekend.

Additionally, OPTIMA Batteries and the Golden State Foods Foundation wrapped up their final OPTIMA Build-A-Bike event of the year at the famed Shelby Museum, a stop on the Detroit Speed and Engineering/JRI Shocks Road Rally. The OPTIMA Invitational participants cheered along as volunteers assembled bicycles along with 50 children from the local Boys & Girls Club chapter.

OPTIMA Invitational Sponsors

Sponsors of the 2012 OPTIMA Ultimate Street Car Invitational include presenting sponsors K&N Filters and Royal Purple; race event sponsors BFGoodrich, Ridetech, Wilwood Disc Brakes, Lingenfelter Performance Engineering and Detroit Speed and Engineering/JRI Shocks. Additionally, The Roadster Shop, MagnaFlow, RECARO, Centerforce Clutches and Mothers are associate sponsors. Beyond sponsoring the event, all of the performance automotive aftermarket companies provided additional prizing for the top winners in each category and the overall winners, providing a rewarding and memorable experience for all participants involved. For more information on the OPTIMA Ultimate Street Car Invitational participants, official rules and more, visit http://www.optimainvitational.com/.

How Can YOU Enter?

The road to the 2013 OPTIMA Invitational is already underway! If you want a chance to compete in the big show simply enter one of the events listed below. If you are good enough you may earn a "Spirit of the Event" invite to the 2013 Invitational!

• Detroit Speed Southern Slam – Kershaw, SC (April 19-21)
• Faceoff at Road America – Elkhart Lake, WI (June 22-23)
• GoodGuys Des Moines – Des Moines, IA (July 5-7)
• MotorState Challenge – Watersvilet, MI (July 25-27)
• Sandhills Open Road Challenge – Arnold, NE (August 7-11)
• Holley LS Fest – Bowling Green, KY (September 6-8)
• Silver State Classic Challenge – Ely, NV (September 11-15)
• GoodGuys Fort Worth – Fort Worth, TX (October 4-6)

Final Results

The 2012 OPTIMA Invitational top 25 ranking participants are listed below and additional final results can be found online at optimainvitational.com.

1. Mark Stielow (1967 Chevrolet Camaro)
2. Brian Hobaugh (1973 Chevrolet Camaro)
3. Todd Earsley* (2003 Mitsubishi Lancer Evolution 8 GSR)
3. Bret Voelkel* (1933 Ford Coupe)
5. Travis Hill (2013 Nissan GT-R)
6. Steven Rupp (1968 Chevrolet Camaro)
7. Danny Popp (2010 Chevrolet Camaro L28)
7. Kyle Tucker (1970 Chevrolet Camaro)
7. Karl Dunn (2007 Ford SaleenParnelli Jones Mustang)
10. Brian Finch (1972 Chevrolet Camaro)
10. Jim Holloway (2013 Ford Mustang RTR)
12. Phil Gerber (1970 Chevrolet C10 Pickup)
12. Ryan Mathews (1966 Ford Mustang)
14. Bob Bertelsen (1971 Chevrolet Camaro)
15. Rob McGregor (1970 Chevy C10 Pickup)
16. Chris Smith (1967 Chevrolet C10)
17. Joey Seely (1986 Porsche Carrera)
18. Dale Akuszewski (1964 Sunbeam Tiger)
18. Jeff Cleary (1967 Chevrolet Corvette)
20. David Brandt (1969 Chevrolet Camaro)
20. Todd Foust (1965 Ford Mustang Convertible)
22. Todd Rumpke (2010 Chevrolet Camaro)
23. Curt Hill (1972 Chevrolet C5 Blazer)
24. Brad Coomer (1970 Chevrolet C10)
25. Stacy Tucker (1969 Chevrolet Camaro)

*Third place was a tie; Per the rules, Todd Earsley earned the official third place because of his placement in the BFGoodrich Hot Lap Challenge

Buick, Oldsmobile, Pontiac & Cadillac For Sale

1957 Oldsmobile 88, Stunning Off Frame Rotisserie Restoration.
Memory Lane Motors (866) 784-1898
$46,900

1962 Buick Skylark, Rebuilt All Aluminum 215 4 bbl V8, Rebuilt 700R4 4 Speed Automatic.
Memory Lane Motors (866) 784-1898
$12,900

1963 Buick Riviera, Granada Red With White Bucket Seat Interior.
Memory Lane Motors (866) 784-1898
$19,900

1964 Pontiac Catalina, Convertible!! Straight from California. Still has California title.
Classic Cars of SC, Inc. (866) 942-7716
$18,000

1966 Cadillac Calais, This is a nice 2-door hardtop with auto transmission and a V8 engine.
Classic Cars of SC, Inc. (866) 942-7716
$8,500

1966 Pontiac GTO, Convertible 389ci/360Hp "Tri-Power" 3x2 V8 4-Speed!
Humpty Dumpty (866) 370-4999
$69,988

1969 Oldsmobile 442, Fully restored and re-finished in Saffron Yellow w/ Black hood stripes.
Wagner's Classic Cars (888) 399-1151
$38,500

1971 Oldsmobile Cutlass Supreme, W-30 Clone-Frame-off restoration, 455ci. V/8, Ram Air.
Wagner's Classic Cars (888) 399-1151
$38,000

1972 Buick Gran Sport, "Lemans Blue" Arrival Blue GSX Stripes, White Bucket Seats w/Console.
Humpty Dumpty (866) 370-4999
$39,988

1972 Pontiac Le Mans, Ultra rare Pontiac muscle car 1 of 5 to be exact!
Wagner's Classic Cars (888) 399-1151
$115,000

1975 Pontiac Trans Am, 455 HO Original Big-Block, Factory 4-Speed, "Bi-Centenial".
Humpty Dumpty (866) 370-4999
$39,988

1976 Pontiac Trans Am, Stunning "Carousel Red" Factory Finish & Original Phoenix Hood Decal!
Humpty Dumpty (866) 370-4999
$29,988

1981 Pontiac Trans Am, Fresh rebuilt 301 v8, automatic, Dorado Gold finish,w/tan cloth.
Frankman Motor Company, Inc. (888) 673-6515
$19,800

1994 Pontiac Trans Am, 25th Anniversary Edition. Stunning! White GM Factory Finish.
Humpty Dumpty (866) 370-4999
$19,988

Chevrolet For Sale

1933 Chevrolet Custom, All Steel Body With Fiberglass Fenders.
Memory Lane Motors
(866) 784-1898
$24,900

1941 Chevrolet Custom, Approx 25,000 Miles Since Original Build By John Byers.
Memory Lane Motors
(866) 784-1898
$34,900

1947 Chevrolet Sedan, Fresh, Meticulous Frame-Off Resto-Mod With Pictures And Receipts.
Memory Lane Motors
(866) 784-1898
$29,900

1950 Chevrolet Sedan Delivery, "Sedan Delivery" Custom Pro-Built! No Expense Spared!
Humpty Dumpty
(866) 370-4999
$39,988

1952 Chevrolet Fleetline, Featured in Rumble magazine, Super Chevy. winner.
J.J. Rods LLC.
(866) 319-8204
$69,500

1953 Chevrolet 210, Real nice cream and brown paint with tan velour interior.
Classic Cars of SC, Inc.
(866) 942-7716
$15,000

1954 Chevrolet Sedan Delivery, 350-400hp V8 Engine "Stunning" Corvette Velocity Yellow.
Humpty Dumpty
(866) 370-4999
$49,988

1955 Chevrolet 150, Absolutely stunning 150 sedan with power to spare, 632 c.i. Merlin engine.
J.J. Rods LLC.
(866) 319-8204
$125,000

1955 Chevrolet Bel Air, Convertible, 265ci V-8 "Power Pak" Option, Automatic Transmission.
Humpty Dumpty
(866) 370-4999
$119,000

1955 Chevrolet Hardtop, This Pro-Touring custom ground-up build is a beauty. Red interior.
J.J. Rods LLC.
(866) 319-8204
$135,000

1956 Chevrolet 210, Stunning color combination of Silver exterior with Red and White interior.
J.J. Rods LLC.
(866) 319-8204
$95,000

1956 Chevrolet Nomad, Fresh restoration with 200 test miles on this custom Chevy Nomad.
J.J. Rods LLC.
(866) 319-8204
$67,500

1956 Chevrolet Truck, Pro Touring. Outstanding custom with 350 Chevy V8 and Weind supercharger.
J.J. Rods LLC.
(866) 319-8204
$67,500

1958 Chevrolet Impala, Hardtop Sport Coupe, 348 cu.in. Big Block V8 (Original).
Humpty Dumpty
(866) 370-4999
$49,988

1958 Chevrolet Impala, 348 CID Super TurboThrust V8 with Rare "Tri-Power" 3x2 Carbs.
Humpty Dumpty
(866) 370-4999
$79,988

Chevrolet For Sale Continued

1962 Chevrolet Bel Air,
Just completed restoration on a solid "Bubble Top".
Wagner's Classic Cars
(888) 399-1151
$72,000

1962 Chevrolet Corvette,
Matching Number 327/300HP V8, 4 Speed Manual Transmission.
Memory Lane Motors
(866) 784-1898
$56,900

1963 Chevrolet Corvair,
4498 Documented Miles Since New. Completely Unrestored Survivor.
Memory Lane Motors
(866) 784-1898
$19,900

1964 Chevrolet Impala,
S/S 2-DR Hardtop Sport Coupe, Flawless "Tuxedo Black" Mirror Finish.
Humpty Dumpty
(866) 370-4999
$34,988

1964 Chevrolet Impala,
Clean original Atlanta built car, beautiful factory Ember red.
Southern Motors
(866) 631-8863
Call For Price

1964 Chevrolet Malibu,
"PRO-TOUR" 502ci/502Hp Big Block Crate Motor, 5-Speed "Tremic" Trans.
Humpty Dumpty
(866) 370-4999
$39,988

1965 Chevrolet Impala,
Convertible w/ 4 spd. trans. Frame off restoration some time ago.
Frankman Motor Company, Inc. (888) 673-6515
$39,800

1966 Chevrolet Chevelle,
"Pro Touring" features an almost stock appearance with a modern drive-train.
Wagner's Classic Cars
(888) 399-1151
$46,900

1966 Chevrolet Corvette,
California car produced on 12/17/65 in St. Louis plant.
Frankman Motor Company, Inc.
(888) 673-6515
$58,500

1967 Chevrolet C10,
Short-Bed Pickup 327 cu.in. GM V8, Automatic Trans "Factory Air Conditioning"
Humpty Dumpty
(866) 370-4999
$24,988

1967 Chevrolet Chevelle,
Striking red with black interior, 369 Turbo jet motor with automatic trans.
Classic Cars of SC, Inc.
(866) 942-7716
$30,000

1967 Chevrolet Chevelle,
Malibu convertible that has been Cloned to look like an SS.
Classic Cars of SC, Inc.
(866) 942-7716
$30,000

1967 Chevrolet Corvette,
StingRay Convertible with Vinyl Covered Auxiliary Hardtop.
Humpty Dumpty
(866) 370-4999
$79,988

1967 Chevrolet Malibu,
2-Door Sport Coupe "L-79" 327/350 Hp V8 4-Speed Manual Trans
Humpty Dumpty
(866) 370-4999
$32,988

1967 Chevrolet Nova, You are looking at a nice 1967 Chevrolet Nova true SS 2-Door hardtop.
Classic Cars of SC, Inc.
(866) 942-7716
$19,000

Chevrolet For Sale Continued

1967 Chevrolet Nova,
Complete professional restoration on this mild custom Nova hardtop.
J.J. Rods LLC.
(866) 319-8204
$65,000

1968 Chevrolet Camaro,
She has been sitting in storage since 1987 and is ready for her new home!
Classic Cars of SC, Inc.
(866) 942-7716
$20,000

1968 Chevrolet Camaro,
Featured in Super Chevy Magazine centerfold April 2011.
J.J. Rods LLC.
(866) 319-8204
$59,500

1968 Chevrolet Camaro,
One Bad Bowtie, beautiful factory (YY) Butternut yellow, black SS striping.
Southern Motors
(866) 631-8863
Call For Price

1968 Chevrolet Chevelle,
Black on black with a 327, automatic trans, bucket seats, center console.
Classic Cars of SC, Inc.
(866) 942-7716
$20,000

1969 Chevrolet Camaro,
New restoration on this spectacular Pro Touring Camaro.
J.J. Rods LLC.
(866) 319-8204
$65,000

1969 Chevrolet Camaro,
Documented Frame-Off Restoration, beautiful factory (52) Garnet red.
Southern Motors
(866) 631-8863
Call For Price

1969 Chevrolet Camaro,
Here is yet another complete build by Wagner's Classic Cars.
Wagner's Classic Cars
(888) 399-1151
Call For Price

1969 Chevrolet Chevelle,
Recent Frame-Off Restoration, stunning Tangerine metallic paint.
Southern Motors
(866) 631-8863
Call For Price

1969 Chevrolet Corvette,
"StingRay" 427 cu.in. "L89" Aluminum Head "Tri-Power" Big-Block.
Humpty Dumpty
(866) 370-4999
$69,988

1969 Chevrolet Corvette,
"STINGRAY" Convertible "RED -ON-RED" 350ci V-8 4-Speed Manual.
Humpty Dumpty
(866) 370-4999
$39,988

1970 Chevrolet Chevelle,
"S/S" 396-350Hp, 4-Speed Manual Transmission 3:55 Posi.
Humpty Dumpty
(866) 370-4999
$55,000

1970 Chevrolet Chevelle,
Just finished 2 year total restoration every nut, bolt and part replaced.
J.J. Rods LLC.
(866) 319-8204
$37,500

1970 Chevrolet Chevelle,
Clean original Missouri car, factory (14) Cortez silver, black SS stripes.
Southern Motors
(866) 631-8863
Call For Price

1970 Chevrolet Corvette,
"LS-5" 454 cu.in. 390 Hp 4-Speed Manual "Rare" Numbers Matching.
Humpty Dumpty
(866) 370-4999
$49,988

Chevrolet For Sale Continued

1971 Chevrolet C10, Short-Bed "Hugger Orange" Houndstooth Deluxe Interior.
Humpty Dumpty
(866) 370-4999
$19,988

1971 Chevrolet Camaro, "S/S" Pro-Touring Split Bumper 396ci Big Block 4-Speed Hurst.
Humpty Dumpty
(866) 370-4999
$39,988

1971 Chevrolet Camaro, "Z/28" Split Bumper "427" Aluminum Head "Muscle Car"! 4-Speed T-10.
Humpty Dumpty
(866) 370-4999
$39,988

1972 Chevrolet Camaro, This split bumper Camaro features a 496ci. pump gas big block.
Wagner's Classic Cars
(888) 399-1151
$26,900

1978 Chevrolet Corvette, "Indy Pace Car" 15k Actual Miles Documented "Limited Edition" "L48"
Humpty Dumpty
(866) 370-4999
$29,988

1992 Chevrolet Custom, True American Hotrod! Super Straight. Beautiful in Black.
Humpty Dumpty
(866) 370-4999
$17,500

1993 Chevrolet Corvette 40th Anniversary Year. 44,306 Actual Florida Miles! Showroom Condition!
Humpty Dumpty
(866) 370-4999
$16,988

2000 Chevrolet Corvette, Flawless "Triple Black Beauty"! Factory Polished Chrome Wheels.
Humpty Dumpty
(866) 370-4999
$21,500

2010 Chevrolet Camaro, One owner SS Camaro with only 6400 miles, never been in the rain.
J.J. Rods LLC.
(866) 319-8204
$29,900

Dodge For Sale

1964 Dodge 440, Nut And Bolt Ground-Up Resto-Mod On A Rust Free Southern California Car.
Memory Lane Motors
(866) 784-1898
$46,900

1964 Dodge Polara, 2900 miles on Complete Rotisserie Restoration.
Southern Motors
(866) 631-8863
Call For Price

1968 Dodge Dart, Built 440 C.I. BIG BLOCK / Six Pack w/ Automatic.
Frankman Motor Company, Inc.
(888) 673-6515
Call For Price

1968 Dodge Dart GT, True Dart GT, beautiful factory (PP1) red, white vinyl interior.
Southern Motors
(866) 631-8863
Call For Price

1970 Dodge Challenger, Recent Rotisserie Restoration, beautiful orange metallic paint.
Southern Motors
(866) 631-8863
Call For Price

Dodge For Sale Continued

1970 Dodge Charger, Roadster "Brilliant Silver Metallic" 2-Tone, Torch Red Leather interior. 440 V-8.
Humpty Dumpty
(866) 370-4999
$79,988

1974 Dodge Charger, Hard Top survivor in Aztec Gold Poly w/ Lt. Parchment interior.
Frankman Motor Company, Inc. (888) 673-6515
$15,850

2009 Dodge Challenger, "R/T" Loaded! Stunning! "Torred Red" Dark Slate Leather Heated Seats.
Humpty Dumpty
(866) 370-4999
$32,988

Ford For Sale

1923 Ford Model T-Replica, "Stunning" Bright Red with Black Interior.
Humpty Dumpty
(866) 370-4999
$25,000

1934 Ford Woodie, This vehicle has been sold, but, the builder can build you a similar or different one.
Classic Cars of SC, Inc. (866) 942-7716
$60,000

1937 Ford Custom, Outstanding, professional built, new Wild Rod Sedan Delivery.
J.J. Rods LLC.
(866) 319-8204
$119,000

1939 Ford Deluxe Tudor, "Pro-Touring" Ready! Henry Ford Steel! 350 5.7 Liter V8 Engine with Automatic.
Humpty Dumpty
(866) 370-4999
$39,988

1939 Ford Coupe, All steel Resto Rod with perfect body fit and finish. Original detailed Flathead V8.
J.J. Rods LLC.
(866) 319-8204
$39,900

1940 Ford Deluxe, 454 Chevrolet V8, 425 Hp, Air Conditioning, Heat, 100% original Steel Body.
Humpty Dumpty
(866) 370-4999
$75,000

1947 Ford Sporstman Convertible, Very rare in outstanding condition and drives like a dream.
J.J. Rods LLC.
(866) 319-8204
$125,000

1962 Ford Galaxie, "XL500" Rare G-CODE 4006ci/406Hp "Convertible" Numbers Matching.
Humpty Dumpty
(866) 370-4999
$69,900

1963 Ford Thunderbird, Corinthian White W/ original and elegant blue leather interior.
Frankman Motor Company, Inc. (888) 673-6515
$15,800

1964 Ford Galaxie, Documented Frame-Up Restoration, beautiful Wimbledon white paint.
Southern Motors
(866) 631-8863
Call For Price

1966 Ford Mustang, Restored Candyapple Red Mustang With Red Deluxe Pony Interior.
Memory Lane Motors
(866) 784-1898
$14,900

Ford For Sale Continued

1966 Ford Mustang, Fresh restoration, beautiful red paint, 289ci. V/8.
Wagner's Classic Cars
(888) 399-1151
$36,500

1967 Ford Thunderbird, Survivor in factory Diamond Blue finish is truly a beautiful example.
Frankman Motor Company, Inc. (888) 673-6515
$13,850

1968 Ford Galaxie, Convertible in a niceRaven Black finish,red vinyl int,302 v8 2bbl.
Frankman Motor Company, Inc. (888) 673-6515
$18,500

1968 Ford Mustang, Shelby-Wanna-B Convertible has a Sweet running Windsor 351.
Classic Cars of SC, Inc.
(866) 942-7716
$35,000

1968 Ford Mustang, PPG Aqua Bluefinish & clear w/ Black interior and nice vinyl buckets.
Frankman Motor Company, Inc. (888) 673-6515
$16,800

1968 Ford Mustang, "True Pro Street"! Paint & Body Total Frame Off rotissery Restoration.
Humpty Dumpty
(866) 370-4999
$39,988

1970 Ford Mustang, Clean Virginia car, True Mach 1, beautiful factory Grabber blue.
Southern Motors
(866) 631-8863
Call For Price

1980 Ford Pro-Street Pinto, 100% street legal Pro Street Pinto!
Wagner's Classic Cars
(888) 399-1151
$21,500

1988 Ford Mustang, 5.0L Engine, 5-Speed Manual FINEST '88 "GT" IN THE WORLD!
Humpty Dumpty
(866) 370-4999
$14,988

1994 Ford Ranger V8, 5.0L V8 "Splash" Pro-Built Pickup. 306ci V8 T5 5-Speed Manual.
Humpty Dumpty
(866) 370-4999
$16,988

1999 Ford Mustang, "COBRA" Rare "SVT" Supercharged V8 5-Speed Transmission.
Humpty Dumpty
(866) 370-4999
$14,988

2007 Ford Mustang, Like new two owner GT Mustang that has never been in the rain.
J.J. Rods LLC.
(866) 319-8204
$20,900

Other Makes For Sale

1941 Willys Custom, Fresh professional built Swoopster with 468 big block Chevy engine.
J.J. Rods LLC.
(866) 319-8204
$75,000

1948 Jeep-Willys Jeepster, California Roadster "Fully Restored" now in Sunny Florida!
Humpty Dumpty
(866) 370-4999
$39,988

Other Makes For Sale Continued

1955 GMC Pickup, Pro Touring Truck. Big back window pickup with a 1957 Chevy grille and dash. *J.J. Rods LLC.* *(866) 319-8204* $135,000

1964 Studebaker Gran Turismo Hawk, Only 1,767 were made !! *Frankman Motor Company, Inc.* *(888) 673-6515* $38,500

1965 AC Cobra, "BackDraft" Roadster, Roush 402R V-8 Engine, Tremec T-56 Six-Speed. *Humpty Dumpty* *(866) 370-4999* $69,988

1965 Volkswagen Beetle, 2167cc. "Big Bore", dual carburetors, Scatt crank & rods, Mahle pistons. *Wagner's Classic Cars* *(888) 399-1151* $21,500

1978 Jeep CJ-7, This 4x4 Jeep spent all its life in California and is in great shape. *J.J. Rods LLC.* *(866) 319-8204* $37,500

2003 Mercedes Benz 500SLR, Silver Ice Metallic w/Charcoal Supple Leather Interior. *Humpty Dumpty* *(866) 370-4999* $29,988

2003 Mercedes Benz SL55 AMG, "Flawless" Black! Charcoal Luxury Napa Leather. *Humpty Dumpty* *(866) 370-4999* $21,988

TIME TO TAKE CHARGE.

THE OPTIMA® CHARGERS FAMILY OF CHARGERS AND MAINTAINERS

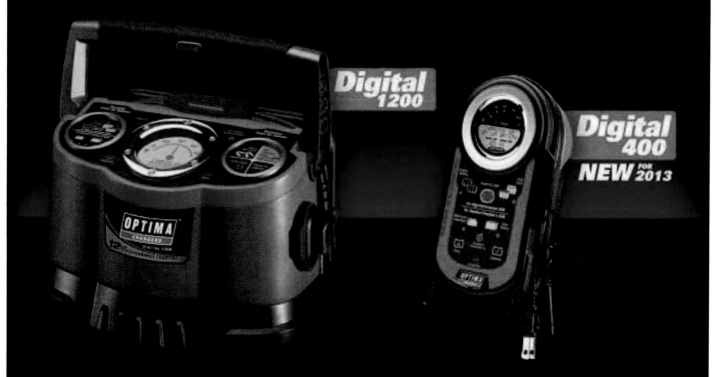

BEST-IN-CLASS FEATURES

Digital 1200

Digital 400

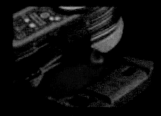

Quick Set Selections
Quick and easy selection of charge profiles by battery type.

USB / Maintenance Port
USB and maintenance charging port for easy, off-season battery maintaining.

Integrated Cable Wrap & Storage
Cable wrap body and reusable cord tie design secures cables for easy storage.

Innovative Multi-Use Design
Dual purpose hook and tilt design allows for in-vehicle hanging or angled stand viewing.

Created by the leader in high-performance AGM batteries, the new OPTIMA Chargers family of products are microprocessor-controlled and will enhance the performance of all types of lead-acid vehicle batteries. They are specifically designed to make AGM batteries carry more power and last longer. They even recover deeply discharged batteries that other chargers can't handle. They charge, condition and maintain all types of 12V flooded and AGM batteries. Stop compromising. It's time to take charge and give your battery high-efficiency charging with OPTIMA Chargers. OPTIMA® CHARGERS. The Ultimate Power Source.™

Now available at participating **Retailers** and optimabatteries.com

Made in the USA
Middletown, DE
19 March 2023

27096749R00029